animal planet™

# Amazing Animal Families

Silver Dolphin

## P1 PRE-LEVEL 1: ASPIRING READERS

## 1 LEVEL 1: EARLY READERS

- Basic factual texts with familiar themes and content
- Concepts in text are reinforced by photos
- Includes glossary to reinforce reading comprehension
- Phonic regularity
- Simple sentence structure and repeated sentence patterns
- Easy vocabulary familiar to kindergarteners and first graders

## 2 LEVEL 2: DEVELOPING READERS

## 3 LEVEL 3: ENGAGED READERS

## 4 LEVEL 4: FLUENT READERS

**Silver Dolphin Books**
An imprint of Printers Row Publishing Group
A division of Readerlink Distribution Services, LLC
9717 Pacific Heights Blvd, San Diego, CA 92121
www.silverdolphinbooks.com

Printers Row Publishing Group is a division of Readerlink Distribution Services, LLC.
Silver Dolphin Books is a registered trademark of Readerlink Distribution Services, LLC.

All notations of errors or omissions should be addressed to Silver Dolphin Books, Editorial Department, at the above address.

ISBN: 978-1-6672-0104-7
Manufactured, printed, and assembled in Heshan, China.
First printing, May 2022. LP/05/22
26 25 24 23 22    1 2 3 4 5

# CONTENTS

# A NOTE TO PARENTS

Learning to read is an exciting time in your child's life! This book will help aspiring readers get started on their journeys.

**All-Star Readers** were created to help make learning to read a fun and engaging experience. Carefully selected stories and subject matter support the acquisition of reading skills, encourage children to learn about the world around them, and help develop a life-long love of books.

This Animal Planet Level 1 collection offers fascinating factual content that is carefully crafted for developing readers. Every child is unique, and age or grade level does not determine a particular reading level. See the previous page for a description of the reading level in this book.

As you read with your child, read for short periods of time and pause often. Encourage them to sound out words they do not know. Suggest they look at the picture on the page for clues about what the word might be. Have younger children turn the pages and point to pictures and familiar words. Each story in this book includes a glossary that defines new vocabulary words. When your child comes across a boldfaced word they don't recognize, instruct them to turn to the glossary and read its definition.

A good way to reinforce reading comprehension is to have a conversation about the book after finishing it. Children love talking about their favorite parts! As your child becomes a more independent reader, encourage them to discuss ideas and questions they may have.

Remember that there is no right or wrong way to share books with your child. When you find time to read with your child, you create a pattern of enjoying and exploring books that will become a love of reading!

# I Am a
# TIGER

Written by Lori C. Froeb

Silver Dolphin

Raaar! I am a tiger cub.

I am small now.

One day I will be a big cat.

Tigers are the biggest cats on Earth!

There are six kinds of tigers alive today.

All tigers live in Asia.

Asia is a large **continent**.

**Bengal tiger**

**Malayan tiger**

# Can you tell us apart?

ASIA

**South China tiger**

**Siberian tiger**

**Indochinese tiger**

**Sumatran tiger**

I am a Siberian tiger.
My family lives in a country called Russia.
Siberia is part of Russia.

We live in the forest.
It can get very cold in winter!

RUSSIA

I live here!

# The world has many big cats.

cheetah

jaguar

tiger

lion

leopard

Siberian tigers are the biggest cats of all.

I will weigh six hundred pounds one day.

My body will be ten feet long from head to tail!

All tigers have striped coats.
Our skin is striped, too.
The stripes are **camouflage**.

They help us blend in
with the grass and trees.

We hide from our **prey**.
We sneak closer until it
is time to pounce.

Tigers are carnivores.
That means we eat meat.

We eat a lot at once.
We do not always eat
every day.

I am too young to hunt.
My mom hunts for our food.
My sister and I watch her.
We will learn to hunt from her.

Most of the time mom hunts for wild boar.

They are pigs with long hair.

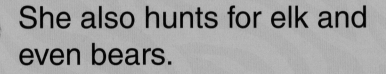

She also hunts for elk and even bears.

Sometimes large prey is hard to find.

Then mom brings us rabbits or fish!

We cannot wait to hunt on our own.

Tigers are expert hunters.
Our bodies are made for it!

## legs

Our back legs are strong.
We can leap thirty feet!

## ears
We can **swivel** our ears to hear prey.

## eyes
We can see very well in day or night.

## teeth
Our teeth can be three inches long. They grip and tear prey.

## feet
Our padded feet are very quiet. This makes it easy to surprise prey.

Adult tigers do not live in groups.

Adult tigers live and hunt alone.

I will stay with my mother until I am two.

Then I will find a **territory** of my own.

A territory is where a tiger lives and hunts.

Tigers mark their territory.
We scratch trees with our nails.
Other tigers see the scratches.

The scratches mean the
area belongs to another tiger.

Our nails can be four inches long!

They are tucked in when not being used.

They stay very sharp.

We also use urine (pee) to mark things.

Mom is not smiling here! She is sniffing the scent left by another tiger.

She opens her mouth to get a better sniff.

She learns about the other tiger.

She can tell if it is male or female and how old it is.

I try to sniff, too!

Most cats do not like the water.

Tigers are not like most cats.

We like the water!

We play in the water and take baths.

Tigers are also great swimmers. Some have swum miles to cross rivers.

We also use sound to talk to each other.

A tiger's roar can be heard two miles away!

We can also growl and hiss. We cannot purr like house cats.

Not all tigers are orange.

Some tigers are white.

All white tigers are Bengal tigers.

White tigers have blue eyes.
About one white tiger is born out of ten thousand cubs.

No white tigers are born or live in the wild.

There used to be many tigers in the wild.

Now there are fewer than four thousand left.

Our **habitats** are shrinking.

Humans hunt us.

We are **endangered**.
This means we may
one day disappear.

If humans protect us, we
will survive.

We will rule the jungle
once again!

# Glossary

**camouflage:** an animal's coloring that helps it hide and blend in

**continent:** one of seven large pieces of land on earth

**endangered:** almost none left in the world

**habitat:** the place where an animal lives

**prey:** an animal that is hunted by other animals for food

**swivel:** to move in different directions

**territory:** the area where an animal lives and hunts

# I Am a
# POLAR
# BEAR

Written by Lori C. Froeb

Silver Dolphin

Hi there! Welcome to my chilly home.

I am a polar bear and these are
my cubs.

The Arctic is the northernmost part of Earth.

Winters are long, dark, and cold.

Summers are short and cool.

# Polar bears live in several places in the Arctic.

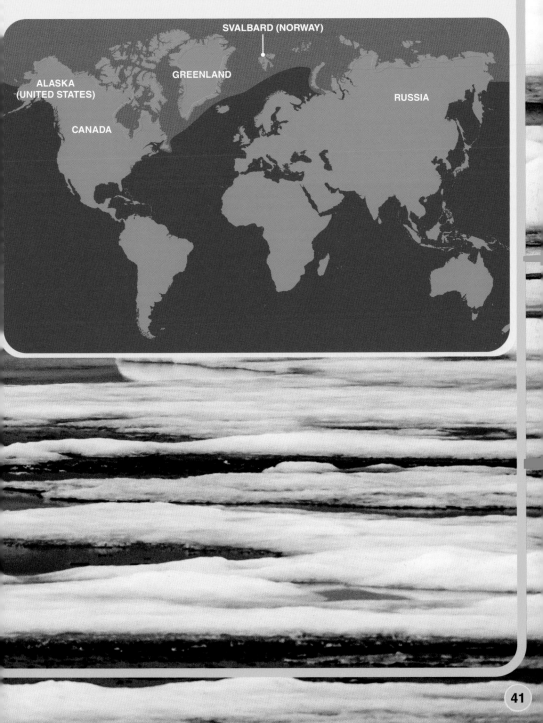

SVALBARD (NORWAY)

GREENLAND

ALASKA
(UNITED STATES)

RUSSIA

CANADA

The temperature in the Arctic can drop to minus fifty degrees in winter.

But I am not cold.

Like all polar bears, I have very thick fur.

My fur is very warm.
It provides good **camouflage**.

I am hard to spot if I am lying
still in the snow.

My fur looks white, but each strand is clear.

Under my fur, my skin is black.

The black color absorbs light from the Sun and warms me up!

My body has another way of staying warm: **blubber**!

Blubber is fat. I have a layer of blubber under my skin.

It is four inches thick in places.

Sometimes I roll in the snow to clean myself. Clean fur is warmer than dirty fur.

Polar bears are more likely to be too hot than too cold. I can cool off in the water.

Polar bears are great swimmers!

We are able to swim for days.

Look at my front paws.
They are as big as
dinner plates.

I use them like giant paddles.

My big paws are great for walking on snow and ice, too.

The bottoms of my paws are covered with tiny bumps.

The bumps grip the slippery ice.

Polar bears are **marine mammals**.

sea otter

polar bear

dolphin

bearded seal

Dolphins, sea otters, and seals are also marine mammals.

Polar bears are the largest **predators** with four legs.

Male polar bears can weigh as much as ten adult humans.

Females like me are much smaller.

Polar bears spend most of their lives on sea ice.

Sea ice is frozen ocean water.

I travel and rest on pieces of sea ice.

I also use the sea ice to hunt for seals.

Seals swim in the water below the ice. They come up to holes in the ice to breathe.

I can smell a seal from a mile away.

I follow my nose to the hole.

Then I wait quietly.

When a seal pops up to breathe, I quickly grab it.

My cubs learn how to hunt from watching me.

Sea ice is around from fall to spring.

During that time, we eat as many seals as we can.

The seals' blubber makes us fat.

When the sea ice melts in the summer, we move to shore.

There is less food to eat on shore.

Sometimes a whale **carcass** washes up on the beach.

This carcass was a lucky find.

Sometimes a hungry polar bear hunts a musk ox or reindeer.

Some polar bears eat seaweed or birds.

None of these things are as good for us as seals.

Many of us eat nothing for months.

We live off our fat until fall.

Earth is warming up, and it is taking longer for sea ice to form.

We are spending more time on land.

Our numbers are getting smaller.

If we do not find a way to survive, we will be **endangered**.

My cubs are strong.

I take good care of them.

I ate a lot of food in the spring before they were born.

I gained more than four hundred pounds!

In the fall, I dug a den in the snow.

I went into the den and rested.

Polar bears don't **hibernate** like other bears.

I did not move much and did not eat for seven months.

Polar bears usually have one, two, or three cubs.

I had two. Twins!

They were born in winter with their eyes closed.

They each weighed less than two pounds.

That is about as much as a small rabbit.

They drank my milk and grew quickly.

In the spring, we left the den.

The cubs learned to walk, swim, and play.

I finally got something to eat.

It had been seven months since my last meal!

Now the cubs watch me hunt on the sea ice.

I smell a seal nearby. It is time for the cubs' lesson.

See you later!

# Glossary

**blubber:** a layer of fat that marine animals use for warmth and energy

**camouflage:** an animal's coloring that helps it hide and blend in

**carcass:** a dead body, usually of an animal

**endangered:** almost none left in the world

**hibernate:** to go into a deep sleep for the winter. Animals don't eat or drink while hibernating.

**marine mammal:** mammals that depend on the ocean to live. Whales, polar bears, and sea otters are marine mammals.

**predator:** an animal that hunts other animals for food

# I Am a
# GORILLA

Written by Lori C. Froeb

Silver Dolphin

Hello! Welcome to Africa.

I am a gorilla.

There are two kinds of gorillas. They all live in Africa.

Western gorilla live in rain forests and marshes.

They live in Cameroon, Gabon, and a few other countries.

**western gorilla**

**AFRICA**

**eastern gorilla**

Eastern gorillas live in mountain forests.

They are found in Rwanda, Uganda, and the Congo.

I am an eastern gorilla.

Gorillas are great apes.

Bonobos, orangutans, and chimpanzees are also great apes.

Apes do not have tails.

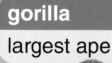

**gorilla**
largest ape

**bonobo**
most peaceful ape

**Monkey, not an ape!**

Monkeys have tails.

**orangutan**

spends most of its life in trees

**chimpanzee**

closest **relative** to humans

Most apes live in Africa.

Orangutans live in Asia.

Look at me.

Do you think you and I look a little alike?

Humans and all apes are **primates**.

Monkeys are primates, too.

Primates have big brains and eyes that face forward.

Primates also have long fingers and toes.

Most primates have **opposable thumbs**.

This means we can use our thumbs to grasp things.

Humans and gorillas mostly have the same DNA.

DNA is in all our cells.

It makes us what we are.

No wonder we look a little alike!

You are part of a family.

I am, too.

My mom and I are part of a **troop**.
A troop is a group of gorillas.

My dad is in charge of the troop. He is a silverback.

The hair on his back turned silver when he became a teenager.

When I get older, I will be a silverback, too.

Dad decides where we look for food.

If there is a fight, Dad breaks it up.

Most times there are no fights.

But Dad is always on the lookout for trouble.

If he sees a male gorilla he does not know, he may roar.

Sometimes he will beat his chest.
This means, "I am in charge."

The number of gorillas in the wild is shrinking.

Humans are the biggest danger to us.

Humans hunt and capture gorillas.

They destroy gorilla **habitats**.

Today, all gorillas are **endangered**.

Gorillas use twenty-five sounds to **communicate**.

We can scream if we are angry or scared.

We hum when we eat.

A hum means we are happy.

A mother gorilla can make a grunting sound.

The sound tells her baby he is doing something wrong.

All gorillas walk using their knuckles and legs.

Our arms are very strong and much longer than our legs.

We can stand and walk on our feet, too.

Now it is time to eat!

Eastern gorillas are **herbivores**.

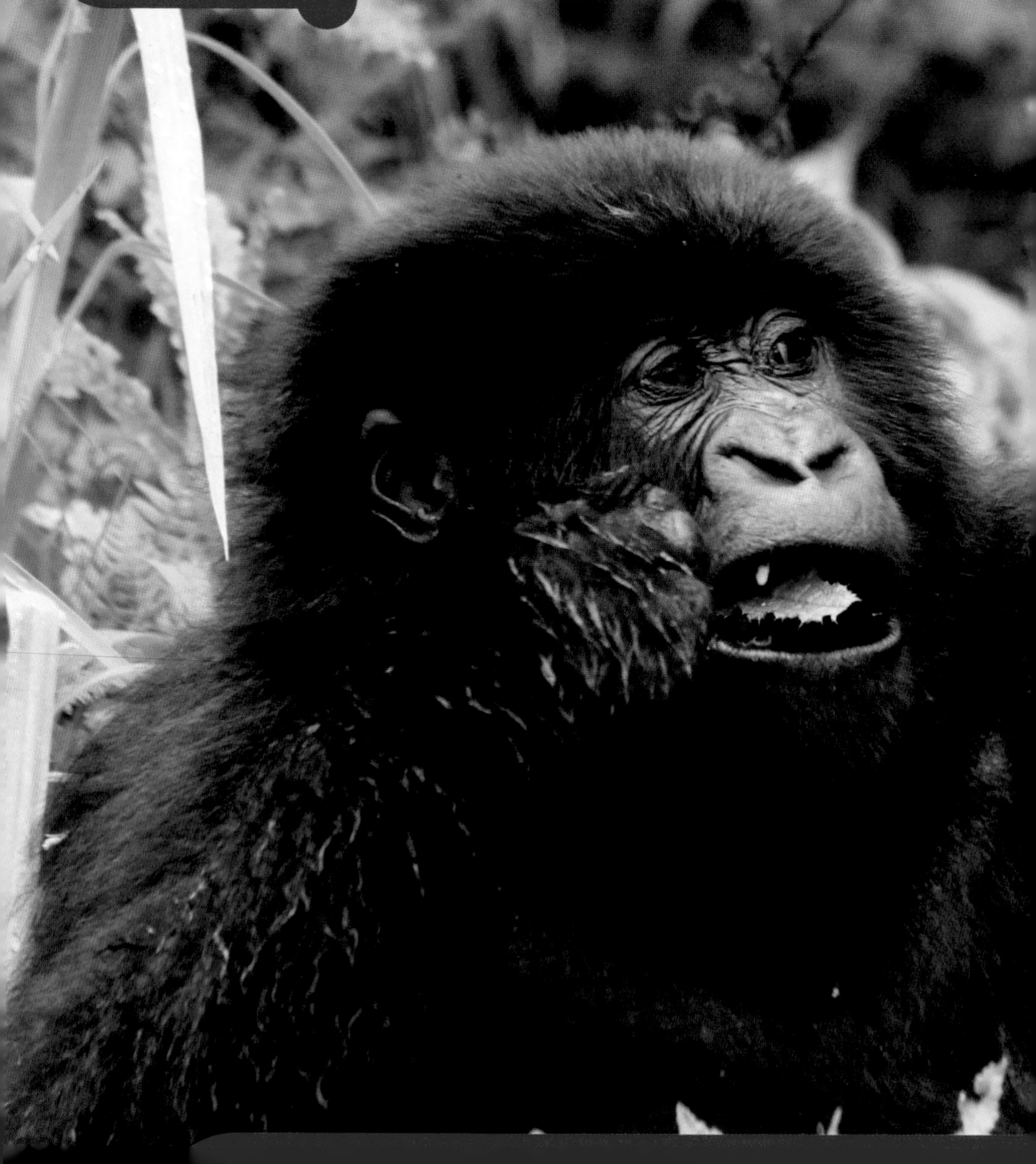

We spend all morning looking for food. Then we eat and take a nap.

When we wake up, we look for food again.

Western gorillas are also mainly herbivores.

They eat a lot of fruit.

When fruit is hard to find, these gorillas eat leaves and bark.

Some also like to eat ants and termites.

ant

bark

termite

leaves

All this looking for food and eating has made me sleepy.

It is time for a nap!

Mom finds branches and leaves.

She makes a nest for us on the ground.

We make a new nest every time we sleep.

I am learning how to make a nest from my mom.

After naptime, I like to play with my friends.

We climb trees, swing from branches, and wrestle.

Sometimes we even play tag!

Gorillas learn from playing.

We learn how to get along with others.

We also learn how to use our arms to swing.

My friends want me to play right now.

See you later!

# Glossary

**communicate:** to share information, ideas, and feelings

**endangered:** almost none left in the world

**habitat:** the place where an animal lives

**herbivore:** an animal that eats only plants

**opposable thumbs:** thumbs that can be used to grasp and hold things

**primate:** a type of mammal that has hands that can grasp, forward-facing eyes, and large brains for their size

**relative:** someone who came from the same ancestor

**troop:** a group of gorillas

# I Am a
# PENGUIN

Written by Lori C. Froeb

Silver Dolphin

Hi there! I am a penguin.
This is my family.
We are emperor penguins.

There are around eighteen **species** of penguins.

Emperor penguins are the largest species.

I am a male emperor penguin.

I weigh about sixty pounds. That is about the same as an eight-year-old human.

I am about four feet tall.

We live where it is very cold.
It is a place called Antarctica.
Antarctica is at the South Pole.

**Galapagos penguin**

Equator

**Chinstrap penguin**

**Magellanic penguin**

Most penguin species live south of the **equator**.

Only the Galapagos penguin lives north of the equator.

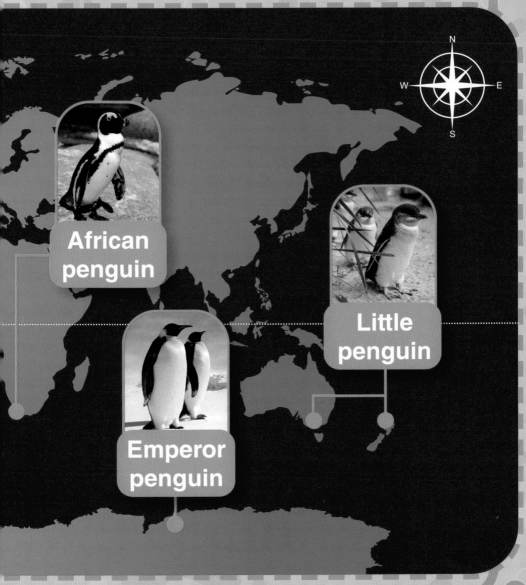

African penguin

Little penguin

Emperor penguin

Not all penguins live in cold places.

This penguin lives in Africa.

It makes a sound like a donkey.

The smallest penguin lives in Australia and New Zealand.

It is called a little penguin.

Little penguins are only about one foot tall.

They are blue and white.

Penguins are birds, but we cannot fly.

Half of our time is spent in the water.

We use our wings as flippers to swim.

Small penguins stay near the surface.

Large penguins like me can dive deep.

I can hold my breath for about twenty minutes!

Penguins are **carnivores**.
We hunt small animals in
the ocean.

squid

krill

My favorite food is fish.
I also eat squid and tiny
animals called krill.

Our mouths are spiny and rough inside.

Slippery fish cannot get away.

Penguins do not chew their food.

We swallow our food whole.

We are quick in the water.
But we are slower on land.
We have short legs and waddle as we walk.

We can move quicker if we hop.

Sometimes we slide on our bellies.

We use our feet to push us forward.

All penguins are covered with thick feathers.

Our feathers are very close together.

They trap air near our skin.

This keeps us warm in the water and on land.

Feathers wear out.

Penguins **molt** at least once a year.

During a molt, all of a penguin's feathers fall out.

New feathers replace the old ones.

My mate and I live in a **colony**.

A colony is a group of penguins.

Our colony sometimes has one thousand birds.

We all nest and hunt together.

This year my mate and I had a chick.
It was hard work!

I met my mate in April.

April is the beginning of winter in Antarctica.

It is a very cold time to lay an egg.

There is ice on the ground.

My mate laid her egg in May.
She carefully placed the egg
on my feet.

The egg could not touch the ice.
The chick inside would freeze.

I balanced the egg on my feet.
I tucked it under my tummy pouch.
The egg was safe and warm there.

Then my mate left to hunt
for food.

I did not see her for two months.

But I was not alone.

All the dads in my colony stuck
together.

We huddled close to stay warm in the wind.

We took turns being on the cold outside.

I protected the egg for sixty-four days.

I did not eat.

I made sure my egg stayed warm.

Then one day the egg hatched!

The chick still had to be kept warm. She stayed on my feet under my pouch.

I fed the chick a liquid from my throat.

Finally, the mother penguins returned.

Some walked over fifty miles back to the colony.

My mate called to me and I answered.

I was so happy to see her!

Then it was my turn to look for food.

While I was gone, my mate fed the chick.

She **regurgitated** food from her stomach.

The chick was always hungry!

We took turns caring for the chick.

She grew fast!

Now our chick huddles with her friends while we hunt.

This group of young penguins is called a **creche**.

I hear my chick calling.
It is my turn to feed her.
Thank you for visiting!

# Glossary

**carnivore:** an animal that eats meat

**colony:** a group of animals living together

**creche:** a group of young animals that stay together for warmth

**equator:** an imaginary line around Earth that is halfway between the North and South Poles

**molt:** when feathers fall out to make room for new ones

**regurgitate:** to bring food up out of the stomach

**species:** a group of living things different from all other groups